Hi, my name is Ethan. time ago the United States of America thirteen colonies ruled by Great Britain?

On July 4, 1776, Wee the People of those colonies wrote a very special document called "The Declaration of Independence."

The British were very angry because we wanted our freedom and war was declared.

Let's go to my home where this story begins and see what brave men and women did to give us freedom today.

1

Said my father to my mother,

"My Dear, as you know, there is a price attached to freedom and this is what we must do to pay.

"We are going to fight people who do not want us to be free, and we must be ready to do this each and every day.

"Now, I am a man who has only a minute to say good-bye, but our story must be told if anyone asks you why.

"Tell them that I go now to war so we can all be free. Explain to them that I do this for you and our children with my head held up high."

2

My mother said,

"We will miss you my dear, and we will pray that God keeps you safe so that you come home to us. We will be waiting for you here.

"This is a burden we all must share. Now, do what you must do.

"I will take care of our wee boy and girl, and remember, we all love you."

3

Ethan thought about what his mother and father said and realized that he was Wee, like "Wee the People" who would write the United States Constitution too.

He thought to himself,

"I will use MY feather made into a pen and tell you what life was like before we went to war and how this country began.

"With great respect and honor, I will tell you about men like my father who was a Minuteman."

So, Ethan began his story and now you will learn more about life and the way it was back then.

On July 4, 1776 this country was part of Great Britain under the rule of old King George.

The relationship between our country and the king was not good.

So, we talked about starting a new country where everyone is free.

We heard the king say,

"If you do that, I will send my soldiers dressed in red coats to stop you. You will never be free. Your country will always belong to me."

Wee the People declared,

"Let us come together and discuss what the king had to say."

Everyone was serious about this matter because it was not a time to play.

In the end, we voted to wage a war against Great Britain.

It was the only way to secure freedom which is our God given right.

So, we gathered at Independence Hall in Philadelphia and gave Thomas Jefferson a feather made into a pen.

Imagine a feather that became mightier than a sword because of what it would write.

There was excitement in the air as we watched him put down on paper everything that Wee the People knew was right.

And this is what he wrote:

Wee the People looked up at the sky with thanksgiving in our hearts thanking God who created us to be free.

We were so grateful for everything that God had given us, and grateful people we should always want to be.

We should call upon God to help us in all that we do, even in little things because they matter too.

We also knew it was right to treat others as we would have them treat us for this was nothing new.

We knew this was good, and you know it too, because good things will forever and always be true.

8

Just like the pilgrims before us we came together with family and friends to worship God as we want because we are free.

We can do this because God blessed our great country with a treasure called liberty.

The king thought he had a mighty hand upon our country, but Wee the People knew we were covered by the hand of God.

We were quick to inform King George that we were going to live our lives as God said we can do.

If we kept God's laws this would always be true.

9

We will tell you now about the treasures in our plan that you will not find unless you live in a land where all people are free under God's blue sky.

After all, this priceless gift is not worth anything unless everyone can have it including you and I.

We created a treasure map that we called "The Declaration of Independence".

Our new leaders were enthusiastic to sign it because freedom was very important so they were sure to be in attendance.

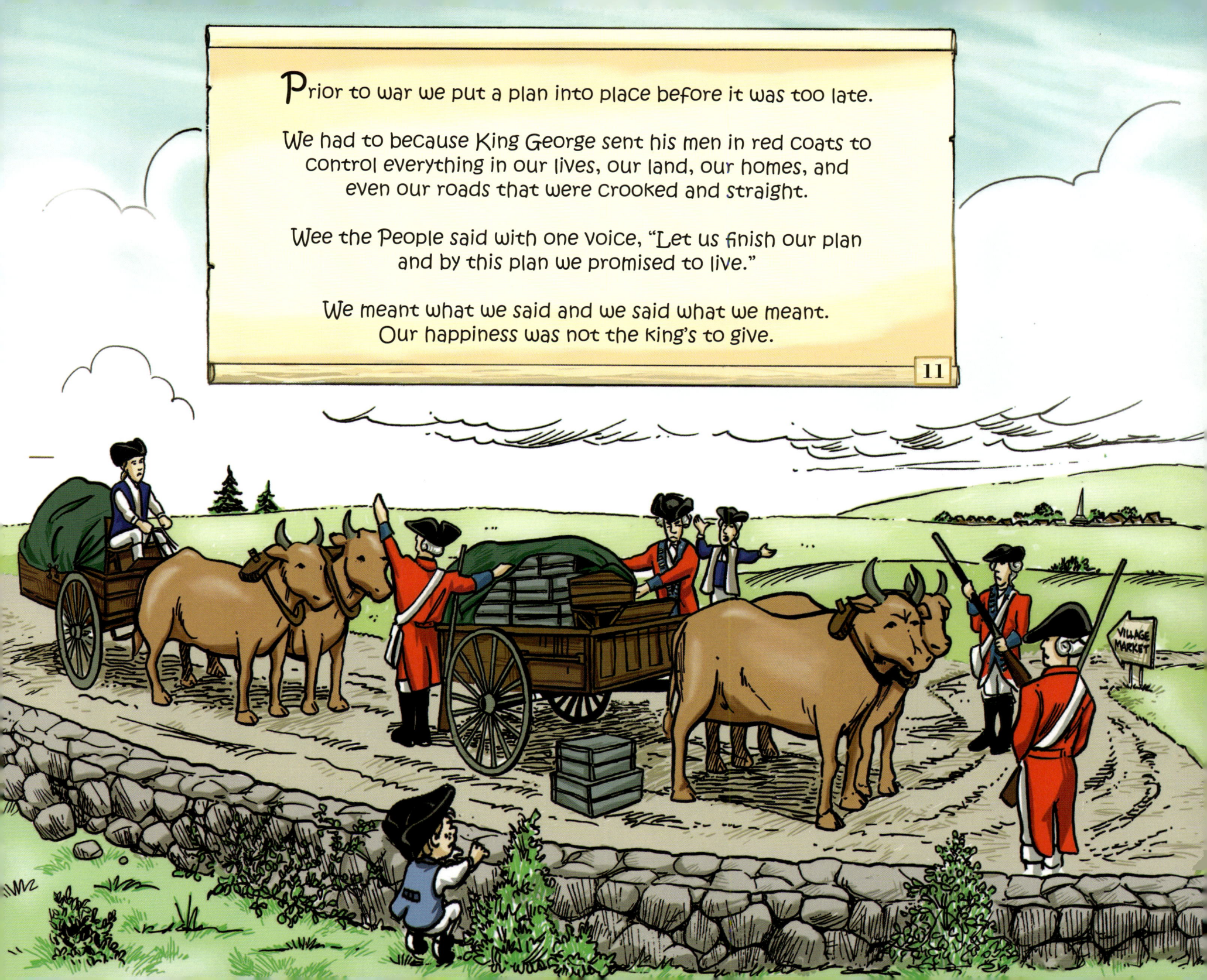

Prior to war we put a plan into place before it was too late.

We had to because King George sent his men in red coats to control everything in our lives, our land, our homes, and even our roads that were crooked and straight.

Wee the People said with one voice, "Let us finish our plan and by this plan we promised to live."

We meant what we said and we said what we meant. Our happiness was not the king's to give.

11

We would work hard under God's good sun but that does not mean everyone's work would be equal when it was done.

Our work might not even be the same, but we know that everyone has special talents and we should do our best regardless of our name.

We would do our best always and everywhere without any shame because it was the right thing to do. God does not judge us as good according to money or fame.

We even wrote down laws that we would live by to make living fair for all.

God does not care about the color of our skin or if we are very short or tall.

And freedom is freedom for everyone no matter how big or small.

13

We said, "God's stamp of freedom is on everything in creation."

We shouted, "We will not listen to you, Mr. King. Whether you like it or not we intend to start a new nation."

This made the king very, very mad.

We did not care, though, because we would be free even if the actions of the king made us very sad.

We suffered; we did, because of the king. He tried to bribe us and threaten us but we would not budge.

We would be happy and free under God our King because God is the highest judge.

We said to the king,

"We will pick our own leaders now, ones who listen to us. We will have no more leaders that Wee the People cannot trust."

We included in our treasure plan the ability to judge our new leaders and if they were not doing their jobs we could send them away.

We told them, "You are no better than us and you must follow the law just as we do. They are laws we all must obey."

So, we must vote them out and they can lead us no more because bad leaders they would continue to be.

If our leaders became really bad we could start this country again by choosing new leaders who might even be you and me.

No matter what happened, no matter what came our way, we were going to be happy and free because this is how God wants us to be.

We have to be very, very careful, though, before we even think about starting this country again, because changing is never an easy thing to do.

If we went down the road of starting this country again there would be a lot of dangerous things to stop us along the way. It would be very difficult to travel this road and make it all the way through.

We received an order from King George and this is what he said, "I, King George, declare that your new leaders will not help the Wee People in any way. I forbid your new laws in America to have any power."

We told King George that we would not listen to him, not even for an hour.

Before we declared war, it was very important to tell everyone about the terrible things that King George did to us just because we wanted to be free and safe at home.

So, Ethan drew up a list of naughty things the king did that would forever and always be known.

King George only pretended he wanted to hear about all the things that made us upset and very sad. We tried to tell him again and again it was because of the things he did to us which were very, very bad. He would not listen to us no matter what we said or did. We gathered in large numbers to call for freedom and even this King George did forbid.

We also knew that King George told his men to take everything that we needed to live. Wee Fathers let the king know our possessions did not belong to him. We needed them to live and for these things our very lives we would give.

We knew that King George tried to make his soldiers more powerful than the laws we made.
To help us fight the king's men, France, Holland and Spain came to our aid.
They also let us borrow money to make sure our bills were paid.

They sent over men and ships to fight with us too, and with the money we
bought cannons, muskets, and gunpowder to defend me and you.

We needed help because King George had sent armies to make us afraid
and to take away our peace. We would not let the king's men scare
us no matter what they did. We would have no bully police.

The king's army committed terrible crimes that no eyes were ever meant to see.

Some of our men were hurt during battle and the king told his men to kill us if we helped our soldiers who fought to make us free.

They even killed our families and friends and the king said his men were free to go home.

And as they left they pushed us down and said, "Fear the king and let it be known."

23

The king's men carried out his commands to burn down our homes, our barns, and everything we owned. We said to the king, "You will do this no more! You have no right to ruin our lives. We will stop you." Our fathers knew what they had to do. They were both rich and poor, but each man fought the king's men for our freedom using his sword and his gun. They would fight side by side when it was cold outside and in the heat of battle under the day's blazing sun.

We had to fight the king's men because he told us that we could no longer buy or sell anything with people from other countries and far away lands. The king even demanded we pay him unfair taxes because he wanted our money in his very greedy hands.

We were told by the king we could no longer judge our own people when we did something wrong.

The king even took our judges back to Great Britain where he put them in prison just because we wanted to be free.

His men would then tease us by playing a haunting song.

And no matter how we pleaded you could hear the sound of a locking key.

HIS ROYAL JUDGERY
KING GEORGE III

WAIT HERE.

We found out King George made up lies to punish us for things we did not even do.

Our fathers said, "King George, your men will feel our muskets and swords. We have surely had enough of you."

More than that, we found out that the king was very sneaky. You see, he asked the people who came to America first to hurt us. This much we knew.

The king would do everything in his power to beat us, but Wee the People knew what we had to do.

The signal that the Redcoats were coming: "One if by land and two if by sea," came from lanterns waved in a steeple up in Boston's Old North Tower.

British ships had made their way to our shores bobbing upon moonlit waves in the dark of the night.

We knew our lives were about to change that very night and hour.

Come what may, Wee the People would be ready for the fight.

28

We heard the clicking and clacking of steel shoes on a horse's feet while running down a cobblestone street. Paul Revere was on a horse named Brown Betty yelling for all to hear, "The British are coming, the British are coming" on a night that was chilly and clear.

With her ears laid back and her nostrils opened big and wide sparks shot out like lightning from her steel shoes while Paul Revere held on for dear life as he went about spreading the news.

29

We went quickly to fight when called, but we would not despise anyone. Bitterness blinds the one who feels that way making it impossible for them to see what is good for you and me.

We would fight our hardest to beat the Redcoats but hatred would have no victory over us because that would make us become like them.

We saw our leaders gather horses and men that we called "Minutemen" because they were ready in a minute's notice to come very quickly when needed with their long bayonet and gun.

We heard our fathers say, "Let us have this war and with this difficult thing be done."

We knew that a battle was coming because the British had finished their plans to fight.

We heard the sounds of men and their muskets as they came from their ships when morning meets night.

Those British Redcoats were stomping their feet in formation as they marched to the beat of their drums on that cobblestone street.

They moved with perfection, not a stumble or trip, but Redcoats or not they could surely be beat.

We watched our brothers go with our fathers to battle, in years they were mere 6 plus 10.

These brothers were not much bigger than Wee Children way back then.

Our mothers gave them food, hugs and kisses knowing their young boys had now become men.

We saw our fathers and brothers praying to prepare their souls in case they were no longer to live.

Then they grabbed their muskets known as squirrel guns to fight for our freedom.

They did this even if it meant that for us their very lives they would give.

April 19, 1775, was the day we Patriots met the British troops at the Lexington Green. It all began there where we stood our ground.

A battle broke out and we lost some men but to our cause we felt duty bound.

The Redcoats then marched to the North Bridge in Concord where our fathers rallied to resist them. It was here a shot rang out heard clear around the world.

Whenever we fight for freedom you can hear the echo of that cracking sound.

In the 8 years that followed we met the Redcoats many times upon the field of battle.

We met them in fields full of hay where we used to play and you could still see some grazing cattle.

We watched them fight the king's men upon the sea as the foaming waves made the boats see saw and sway. Some of our men were captured and told to fight against their own families and friends no matter what they had to say.

Yes, our fathers fought that freedom is not free. night and day, and we must never forget It comes with a price that we all must pay.

We fought so that everyone could live happy and free. Never would we have to go before a king and bow. We wanted everyone to have the right to work so they could have a home that is happy and safe and do things like milk the family cow.

The shots that rang out on Patriots Day led to the birthday of freedom for our new country. We celebrate it on the Fourth of July and have cherished that freedom until this very day. Not only did our fathers fight to make life good and happy for the people back then, but also for the many others that came here after them.

Since George Washington, the Father of our country, we saw our fathers carry the lantern of liberty. For this they fought and some even gave their lives for you and me. Freedom is like a torch that conquers the darkness of oppression when other people do not want us to be free.

War is not to be entered into quickly without a lot of thought. We begged the king again and again to stop doing terrible things, but he would not hear our cries.

We have a name for a man like that king. That name is tyrant which means he is even worse than a very mean bully, a name that he will carry even after he dies.

Although we did not want to fight we learned from all that we suffered that a king's might is not always right.

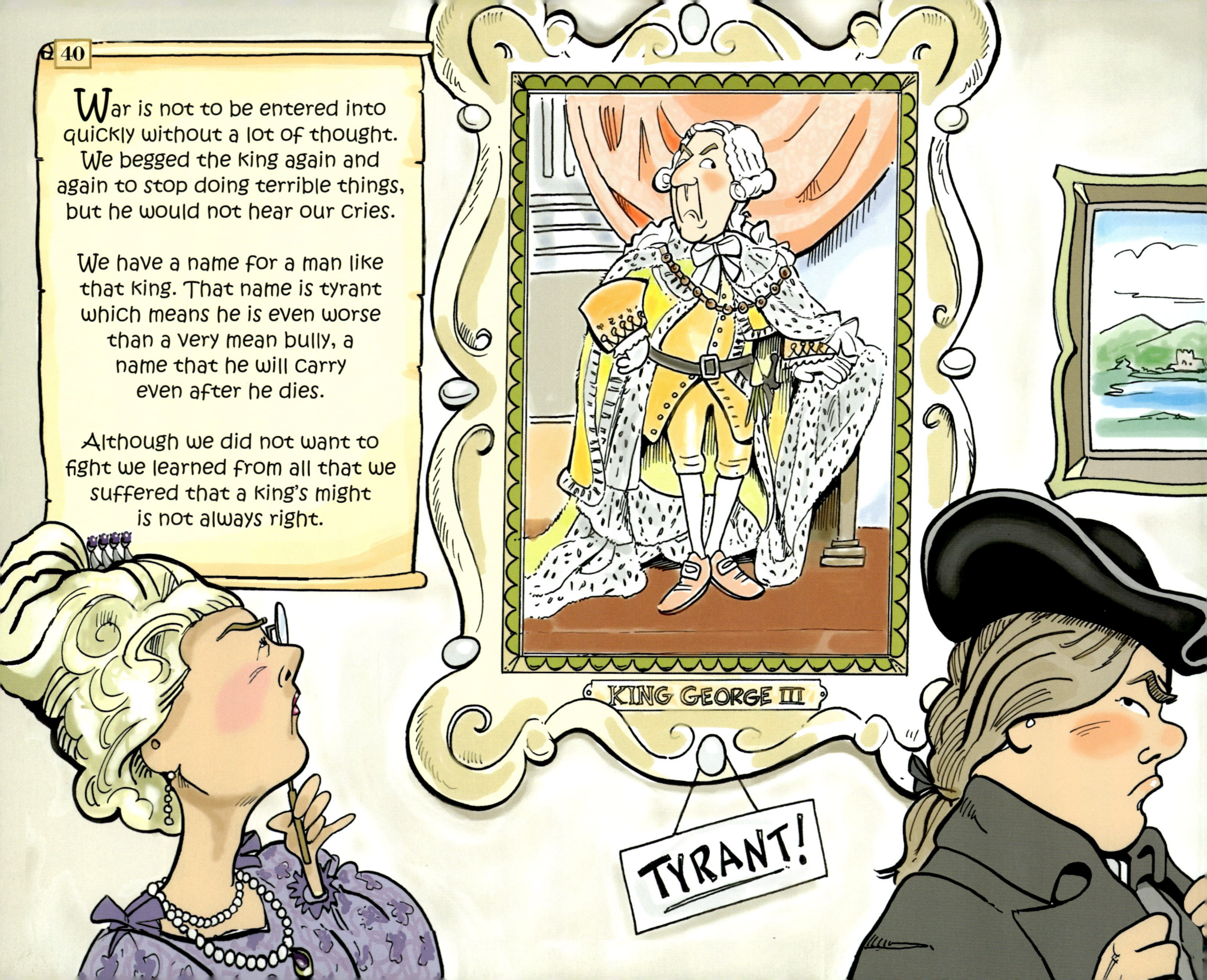

KING GEORGE III

TYRANT!

We even tried to remind the king's men we were friends back in Great Britain, but they waved their muskets in our faces.

We told them that we have muskets too, and that when fighting begins we will pick the places.

Wee the People said with one united voice, "We now see the king's men as our enemy, but they will again be our friends when this war ends."

Then peace there will be across this great land from sea to shining sea.

We finished the plans in our treasure map declaring that Wee the People united under God give our new leaders of the 13 United Colonies permission to start our new nation named the United States of America.

We make it a law that we were free from King George of Great Britain and all of his laws. We would not pay the king anymore taxes. In addition we declare freedom from all other kings and countries all over the world.

We also make it a law that our leaders have nothing to do with leaders loyal to the king.

We are free to make friends, and we can buy and sell goods with people of other countries.

We promise each other to do what we can, and use what we have, to always defend each other. We ask for God's help and protection in this, "The Declaration of Independence."

Signed, Wee the People ...

Delaware - George Read, Caesar Rodney, Thomas McKean
Pennsylvania - George Clymer, Benjamin Franklin, Robert Morris, John Morton, Benjamin Rush, George Ross, James Smith, James Wilson, George Taylor
Massachusetts - John Adams, Samuel Adams, John Hancock, Robert Treat Paine, Elbridge Gerry
New Hampshire - Josiah Bartlett, William Whipple, Matthew Thornton
Rhode Island - Stephen Hopkins, William Ellery
New York - Lewis Morris, Philip Livingston, Francis Lewis, William Floyd
Georgia - Button Gwinnett, Lyman Hall, George Walton
Virginia - Richard Henry Lee, Francis Lightfoot Lee, Carter Braxton, Benjamin Harrison, Thomas Jefferson, George Wythe, Thomas Nelson, Jr.
North Carolina - William Hooper, John Penn, Joseph Hewes
South Carolina - Edward Rutledge, Arthur Middleton, Thomas Lynch, Jr., Thomas Heyward, Jr.
New Jersey - Abraham Clark, John Hart, Francis Hopkinson, Richard Stockton, John Witherspoon
Connecticut - Samuel Huntington, Roger Sherman, William Williams, Oliver Wolcott
Maryland - Charles Carroll, Samuel Chase, Thomas Stone, William Paca

ALL NEW PATRIOTS SIGN HERE: _____
STATE: _____
DATE: _____

43

The unanimous Declaration of the thirteen united STATES of America – for Adult Patriots

When in the Course of human events, it becomes necessary for one people to dissolve the political bands which have connected them with another, *(Pages 2, 28, 29 & 30)* and to assume among the powers of the earth, the separate and equal station to which the Laws of Nature and of Nature's God entitle them, *(Pages 12 & 14)* a decent respect to the opinions of mankind requires that they should declare the causes which impel them to the separation *(Page 6)*.

We hold these truths to be self-evident *(Pages 7 & 8)*, that all men are created equal, that they are endowed by their Creator with certain unalienable Rights, that among these are Life, Liberty and the pursuit of Happiness *(Page 10)*. That to secure these rights, Governments are instituted among Men, deriving their just powers from the consent of the governed, *(Page 9)* —That whenever any Form of Government becomes destructive of these ends, it is the Right of the People to alter or to abolish it, and to institute new Government, laying its foundation on such principles and organizing its powers in such form, as to them shall seem most likely to effect their Safety and Happiness. Prudence, indeed, will dictate that Governments long established should not be changed for light and transient causes; and accordingly all experience hath shewn, that mankind are more disposed to suffer, while evils are sufferable, than to right themselves by abolishing the forms to which they are accustomed. *(Page 17)* But when a long train of abuses and usurpations, pursuing invariably the same Object evinces a design to reduce them under absolute Despotism, it is their right, it is their duty, to throw off such Government, and to provide new Guards for their future security. —Such has been the patient sufferance of these Colonies; and such is now the necessity which constrains them to alter their former Systems of Government *(Page 15)*. The history of the present King of Great Britain is a history of repeated injuries and usurpations, all having in direct object the establishment of an absolute Tyranny over these States *(Page 5 & 41)*. To prove this, let Facts be submitted to a candid world *(Page 19)*.

He has refused his Assent to Laws, the most wholesome and necessary for the public good *(Page 22)*. **He has** forbidden his Governors to pass Laws of immediate and pressing importance, unless suspended in their operation till his Assent should be obtained; and when so suspended, he has utterly neglected to attend to them *(Page 18)*. **He has** refused to pass other Laws for the accommodation of large districts of people, unless those people would relinquish the right of Representation in the Legislature, a right inestimable to them and formidable to tyrants only *(Page 20)*. **He has** called together legislative bodies at places unusual, uncomfortable, and

distant from the depository of their public Records, for the sole purpose of fatiguing them into compliance with his measures *(Page 18)*. **He has** dissolved Representative Houses repeatedly, for opposing with manly firmness his invasions on the rights of the people. **He has** refused for a long time, after such dissolutions, to cause others to be elected; whereby the Legislative powers, incapable of Annihilation, have returned to the People at large for their exercise; the State remaining in the mean time exposed to all the dangers of invasion from without, and convulsions within *(Page 20)*. **He has** endeavored to prevent the population of these States; for that purpose obstructing the Laws for Naturalization of Foreigners; refusing to pass others to encourage their migrations hither, and raising the conditions of new Appropriations of Lands *(Page 38)*. **He has** obstructed the Administration of Justice, by refusing his Assent to Laws for establishing Judiciary powers *(Page 15)*. **He has** made Judges dependent on his Will alone, for the tenure of their offices, and the amount and payment of their salaries *(Pages 15, 18 & 20)*. **He has** erected a multitude of New Offices, and sent hither swarms of Officers to harass our people, and eat out their substance *(Page 21)*. **He has** kept among us, in times of peace, Standing Armies without the Consent of our legislatures *(Page 22)*. **He has** affected to render the Military independent of and superior to the Civil power *(Page 22)*. **He has** combined with others to subject us to a jurisdiction foreign to our constitution, and unacknowledged by our laws; giving his Assent to their Acts of pretended Legislation: